The Urbana Free Library

To renew: call 217-367-4057
or go to *urbanafreelibrary.org*
and select "My Account"

FAKE NEWS

GLOBAL CITIZENS: MODERN MEDIA

Published in the United States of America by Cherry Lake Publishing
Ann Arbor, Michigan
www.cherrylakepublishing.com

Content Adviser: Jessica Haag, MA, Communication and Media Studies
Reading Adviser: Cecilia Minden, PhD, Literacy expert and children's author

Photo Credits: ©ANDRANIK HAKOBYAN/Shutterstock.com, Cover, 1; ©Blend Images/Shutterstock.com, 5;
©Digital Buggu/Pexels.com, 6 ©India Picture/Shutterstock.com, 7; ©y6uca/Shutterstock.com, 8; ©Couperfield/
Shutterstock.com, 10; ©fizkes/Shutterstock.com, 11; ©Freedomz/Shutterstock.com, 13; ©arrowsmith2/
Shutterstock.com, 14; ©Cat Act Art/Shutterstock.com, 15; ©eightshot/Shutterstock.com, 16; National
Archives and Records Administration/Public Domain/Wikimedia Commons, 19; ©Drop of Light/
Shutterstock.com, 20; ©FS Stock/Shutterstock.com, 21; ©Monkey Business Images/Shutterstock.com, 22;
©Natee Meepian/Shutterstock.com, 23; ©Rawpixel.com/Shutterstock.com, 24; ©Lopolo/Shutterstock.com, 27;
©Iam_Autumnshine/Shutterstock.com, 28

Library of Congress Cataloging-in-Publication Data has been filed and is available at catalog.loc.gov

Cherry Lake Publishing would like to acknowledge the work of the Partnership for 21st Century Learning.
Please visit www.p21.org for more information.

Printed in the United States of America
Corporate Graphics

ABOUT THE AUTHOR

Wil Mara has been an author for over 30 years and has written more than 100 educational titles
for children. His books have been translated into more than a dozen languages and won numerous
awards. He also sits on the executive committee for the New Jersey affiliate of the United States
Library of Congress. You can find out more about Wil and his work at www.wilmara.com.

TABLE OF CONTENTS

CHAPTER 1

History: Fake News Then and Now

People have been communicating with each other for thousands of years. What began as rock carvings has slowly changed into books, newspapers, magazines, movies, radio, TV, and the Internet. Together, they are called **media**.

"**Fake news**" is a phrase used to describe a news story that has been released through media and has information that is either greatly exaggerated or completely untrue. The term was popularized during the 2016 U.S. presidential election, but it has been in use in newspapers since the 1890s. The purpose of fake news is to mislead the public. The aim is generally to damage the reputation of a person, group of people, or organization. The goal might also be to make a profit or win political favor.

Sometimes people can confuse satirical news, or news meant to be ironic and humorous, for real news.

From the Beginning

Fake news stories dates back as far as ancient Rome. Mark Antony was one of the leaders during the first century BCE. He was a general and a politician. Octavian, his political rival, spread negative stories about him to the Roman public, portraying him as a traitor. While it was untrue, the Roman people still turned against Antony. Another rumor was spread that his beloved Cleopatra had taken her own life. When he heard this, a heartbroken Antony did the same—never knowing that the claim of her death had been a lie.

The newspaper industry was at its peak in 1984—more than 64 million newspapers were circulating!

The News Industry Takes Shape

The news industry drastically changed in the mid-1400s following the invention of the **printing press**. At the time, newspapers were not guided by any laws or regulations. Fake news could be published by anyone. By the 1600s, however, people had grown tired of being misled and demanded that writers name their **sources**.

Italian philosopher and scientist Galileo Galilei didn't publish fake news, but people thought he did. He was put on trial in

The news industry has almost always mixed entertainment with news reporting.

A story today, real or fake, can go viral with just one click of a button.

1633 because his scientific findings went against public opinion. He discovered that the earth moved around the sun. At that time, people thought the opposite. They believed the sun moved around the earth. Galileo was accused of spreading false information. During the trial, he was forced to provide evidence to support his scientific theories. But even with evidence, he had a difficult time changing people's minds.

Modern Times

We are exposed to media every day—television, print publications, online websites, and social media. With so many outlets, it's easy to plant fake news stories. And it's easy for a story, true or untrue, to go **viral**. One small story released through something as simple as a **tweet** can be shared by thousands of people several different ways.

An example of fake news happened in 2009. An article claimed that FBI director Robert Mueller was part of a scheme to help Russia obtain uranium to use for weapons. Uranium is a dangerous metal. The truth was that Mueller was cooperating

Benjamin Franklin and Fake News

During the Revolutionary War, Benjamin Franklin published fake news! In 1782, he wrote that Native Americans had sent the king of England a bagful of scalps they had cut from the heads of colonists. Franklin wrote the Native Americans were fighting on the king's behalf, and the king was delighted to receive the scalps. As a result, thousands of colonists became more determined than ever to defeat the king's forces and attain American independence.

Some people incorrectly use the term "fake news." They use it to describe news they do not like, journalistic errors, and conspiracy theories.

According to a survey, 64 percent of people feel that the rise of fake news causes confusion about current events.

with Russian authorities on an operation to catch people who were illegally selling it. There's a big difference between the true and untrue stories.

Developing Questions

People generally trust the media to deliver news to them. Many do not realize a story is fake until after it has done its damage. Where do you see the relationship between the general public and the media going in the future? If fake news were allowed to continue, what do you think the media would do to restore public confidence?

CHAPTER 2

Geography: Fake News Is a Global Problem

Fake news is a problem not only in the United States, but also around the world. Because of the Internet and social media, it is easier than ever for a false story to start in one country and spread to the other side of the world in a matter of hours. Countries are working to fight this, but it's not that easy to undo a story that has gone viral.

Politics and the Rise of Fake News

Countries have laws that can help eliminate the practice of creating and releasing fake news. But it still happens, and sometimes people in power use fake news to boost their public standing.

Celebrities, from YouTube vloggers to movie stars, influence their followers.

Political campaigns have been known to exaggerate and even falsify information to sway public opinion. One instance of this happening was in 2010. A special election was being held to fill U.S. Senator Ted Kennedy's seat after he died while in office. Researchers found that one political party paid for Twitter **bots** to spread false information about the candidate from the other party just hours before the election!

Political campaigns aren't the only ones spreading fake news. Celebrities also use their influence to sway public opinion.

The government in Italy is collaborating with journalists, Google, and Facebook to start a program that will teach high schoolers on how to fight fake news.

A famous Filipino singer with 5.4 million followers on Facebook used her social media presence to spread fake news. She did this to **defame** a political candidate she didn't like.

Twitter Bots

*One of the ways **hackers** spread fake news quickly is through the use of Twitter bots. These are essentially computer programs hidden behind fake Twitter accounts. Hackers will use these bots to rapidly spread fake stories and other information to real Twitter users in order to influence their opinion.*

14

In some parts of the world, like in Southeast Asia where Internet access is relatively new to its citizens, Facebook is the main source of news.

BBC surveyed 18 countries and found that 79 percent of people were worried about fake news on the Internet, with Brazilians being the most worried.

The Difficulty of Creating Laws

It can be difficult to walk the fine line between fake news and **free speech**. The right to free speech is guaranteed by many countries, and some people purposely abuse that right. Laws are needed to crack down on those who spin fake news stories. How can we determine when someone goes too far?

In June 2017, the German government passed a law requiring popular media outlets, such as Facebook and Twitter, to do a better job of **monitoring** their sites. Other nations in Europe took similar steps. In the Czech Republic, for example, a special **watchdog** unit was created to read through daily stories on news and social media sites. The team was searching for claims that had no facts to back them up.

Gathering and Evaluating Sources

*Using resources on the Internet and at your local library, determine which countries are being the most **proactive** about stopping fake news within their borders and which are not. Can you determine why some countries are making more of an effort than others? Use the information you find to support your answers.*

CHAPTER 3

Civics: The Effects of Fake News

Fake news presents the world with real dangers. It's one thing for a person to read something false or misleading. It's another thing for that person to accept it and share that information as fact. If fake news is allowed to become widespread, it's only a matter of time before everyone stops trusting anything that's said or written in the news.

Making Important Decisions

The great majority of voters don't know their political candidates personally. They trust the media to deliver factual and unbiased information about them. But people also tend to trust what their friends say or share on social media.

The First Amendment to the Constitution of the United States protects free speech.

France is introducing a law that would allow judges the right to remove reports that were considered fake during election season.

After the 2016 U.S. presidential election, a study found that about 14 percent of voters used social media as their primary source of information. That same study determined that about 115 fake stories in support of candidate Donald Trump were shared on Facebook at least 30 million times. The study reported that roughly 40 fake stories supporting candidate Hillary Clinton were shared over 7 million times. Most of these stories were planted on fake news sites that looked real. This makes it even more difficult for people to determine what is real and what is fake.

Many colleges, like the University of Michigan, now offer courses
to help students combat fake news.

About one in four people get their news from multiple social media sites.

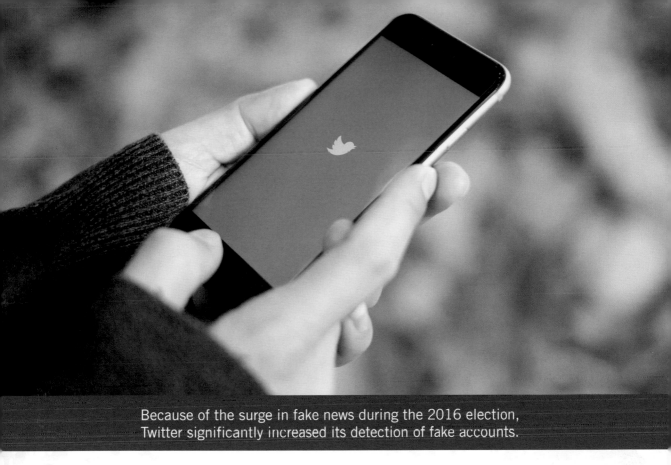

Because of the surge in fake news during the 2016 election, Twitter significantly increased its detection of fake accounts.

Social Media

Many believe that the rise of fake news is mainly due to the rise of social media. Your friends post a story. You share the story, sometimes without reading the article. A lot of fake news was fed through Facebook during the 2016 presidential campaign. Facebook founder Mark Zuckerberg took a lot of heat for this from investigative agencies following the election. It was reported that about 3,000 ads were created by around 470 fake Facebook

According to a study, people are more likely to believe something the more times they read it.

Birth Certificate Conspiracy

Many people falsely claimed that former president Barack Obama wasn't born in America. They said that because of this, he was not legally qualified to be the president in the first place. In truth, he was born in Hawaii. Yet a survey taken in 2017 found that more than 10 percent of the people polled still believed he was born in another country. They still believed this because of a fake news story they had read in the past.

accounts from June 2015 to May 2017. These fake ads were seen by about 10 million users and may have been shared 340 million times! These ads were in clear violation of Facebook's policies, yet they weren't caught until September 2017. Because of this, Facebook plans on creating a better and more secure method of filtering out fake accounts and ads.

Developing Claims and Using Evidence

So-called facts in fake news stories are accepted by some people as truth. These people will then share the misinformation with friends and family. If you are uncertain about the claims made in an article or on a video clip, take the time to look for more evidence that supports or contradicts those claims. Determine which statements are supported by real facts and which statements are opinions made to look like facts. Pay close attention to the news source as well. Is the article or video clip coming from an unbiased source? Or is the source known to lean in a certain political direction?

CHAPTER 4

Economics: The Numbers Behind Fake News

Today, there is an estimated 2.5 billion social media users. That's 2.5 billion people who will potentially see and share fake news! Fake news is a bigger problem now than ever before.

The Heavy Cost of Fake News

A carefully targeted fake news story can immediately affect a company's reputation and its **stock price**. Even after the false story is identified as untrue, the damage may take longer to undo.

A recent example of this occurred in November 2016. It was falsely reported that the head of PepsiCo, Indra Nooyi, said that President Trump's supporters should "take their business elsewhere."

One way to detect fake news is to visit trustworthy fact-checking websites.

Because of this, PepsiCo's stock price dropped dramatically. Despite the story being quickly corrected, PepsiCo's stock price continued to fall. The price reportedly fell more than 5 percent that month.

Real vs. Fake News

According to a survey published by CNN in April 2017, only about 44 percent of young people feel confident that they can tell a real news story from a fake one. Among that 44 percent, 33 percent admitted they had shared a story with their friends that turned out to be fake.

Fake news is like a rumor: The best way to stop false information from spreading is to not share it.

Taking Informed Action

When a media outlet runs a story that sounds questionable to you, ask yourself what the media's reasons might be for running the story. For example, a company that makes over-the-counter drugs may have strong connections to a certain media outlet. If that media outlet runs a story about one of the drug company's products being safe, would you trust it? Why or why not? Questioning the motives behind a story that might sound suspicious is always a good idea.

A Profitable Undertaking

While companies may lose money from fake stories, some people write them to make money. In Veles, Macedonia—a small town of about 44,000 people—teenagers made over $5,000 a month by producing and promoting fake news. In 2016, they created fake articles and news sites that quickly went viral. One teen reportedly made over $60,000 in only 6 months. Another teen reported to have made up to $2,500 in only a day.

Communicating Conclusions

Before reading this book, did you know about fake news? Now that you know more, why do you think it's important to recognize fake stories from real ones? Based on what you've read and the research you've done, what do you think will happen next in the fight against fake news? Use the information you've found to support your answer.

Think About It

More adults than ever before are turning to the Internet for news. A survey conducted by the respected Pew Research Center in August 2017 found that 67 percent of American adults get at least some of their news from online sources. This includes 55 percent of adults who are 50 years old or older. Among online sites, Facebook continues to be the leader of news, with 45 percent saying they go there regularly for news. Just 18 percent go to YouTube for news, and 11 percent go to Twitter.

What does this data tell you about the future of fake news and real news? Who do you think will suffer the most from fake news in the years ahead? Who will benefit?

For More Information

Further Reading

Heitner, Devorah. *Screenwise: Helping Kids Thrive (and Survive) in Their Digital World*. Brookline, MA: Bibliomotion, Inc., 2016.

McKee, Jonathan. *The Teen's Guide to Social Media ... and Mobile Devices: 21 Tips to Wise Posting in an Insecure World*. Uhrichsville, OH: Shiloh Run Press, 2017.

Mooney, Carla. *Asking Questions About How the News Is Created*. Ann Arbor, MI: Cherry Lake Publishing, 2016.

Websites

Common Sense Media—News and Media Literacy
https://www.commonsensemedia.org/news-and-media-literacy/how-can-kids-figure-out-whats-credible-news-and-whats-fake-news
Read how you can tell the difference between real and fake news.

National Geographic Kids—Spotting Fake News
https://kids.nationalgeographic.com/explore/ngk-sneak-peek/april-2017/fake-news
This excellent site gives details on how kids can uncover fake news.

GLOSSARY

bots (BAHTZ) hidden software programs that performs massive online functions at great speed and in great quantity

defame (dih-FAME) to harm someone's reputation by making false charges about that person

fake news (FEYK nooz) news that is published or broadcast with the intent to mislead people in order to destroy the reputation of a person, group of people, or organization

free speech (FREE SPEECH) the right to speak, write, or otherwise communicate freely about what is on your mind

hackers (HAK-erz) people who undertake illegal computer-related activity, usually with the aid of the Internet

media (ME-dee-uh) a method of communication between people, such as a newspaper

monitoring (MAH-nih-ter-ing) constantly watching something in order to prevent problems

printing press (PRINT-ing PRESS) a device designed to print ink onto paper in large quantities

proactive (proh-AK-tiv) taking action to prevent problems that are expected to happen

sources (SORS-iz) places where information is taken from or originates

stock price (STAHK PRISE) a portion of a company that you buy for a certain price as an investment

tweet (TWEET) a posting on the social media website Twitter with thoughts or information

viral (VYE-ruhl) quickly and widely spread or popularized, especially by means of social media

watchdog (WAHCH-dawg) a person or group of people who make sure companies or governments do not do anything illegal

INDEX